discover countries

France

D1080990

Susan Crean

PERMANENTLY WITHDRAWN
FROM
HAMMERSMITH AND FULHAM
PUBLIC LIBRARIES

PRICE

WAYLAND

HAMMERSMITH AND FULHAM

3 8005 01552 958 4

Printed in 2012

Wayland
Hachette Children's Books
338 Euston Road
London NW1 3BH

Wayland Australia
Level 17/207 Kent Street,
Sydney, NSW 2000

All rights reserved

Editor: Paul Manning
Designer: Paul Manning
Consultant: Rob Bowden

Produced for Wayland by
White-Thomson Publishing Ltd

www.wtpub.co.uk
+44 (0)845 362 8240

Crean, Susan.
France. -- (Discover countries)
1. France--Juvenile literature.
I. Title II. Series
944'.084-dc22

ISBN: 9780750267045

Printed in China

Wayland is a division of Hachette Children's Books
an Hachette UK company
www.hachette.co.uk

First published in 2010 by Wayland
Copyright © Wayland 2010

This paperback edition published by Wayland in 2011

Reprinted in 2012

All data in this book was researched in late 2009
and has been collected from the latest sources available at that time.
Please note that figures refer to 'metropolitan' France and do not include
overseas territories belonging to the French Republic.

Picture credits
Front cover l, Shutterstock/Marc Pagani Photography; front cover r, Shutterstock/Peter Kirillov;
1, Shutterstock/Marc Pagani Photography; 3t, Shutterstock/Cristina Ciochina; 3b, Shutterstock/Knud Nielsen; 4 (map), Stefan Chabluk;
5, Shutterstock/Paul Campbell; 6, Shutterstock/David Hughes; 7, Shutterstock/©photazz; 8, Shutterstock/rixxo; 9, Corbis/Owen Franken;
10, Mikhail Zahranichny; 11, Corbis/Fridmar Damm; 12, Corbis/Philippe Lissac; 13, Corbis/Pierre Jacques; 14, Corbis/Philippe Lissac;
15, Corbis/Pascal Deloche; 16, UPPA/Photoshot; 17, Corbis/Owen Franken; 18, Corbis/John Harper; 19, Air France; 20, Corbis/Frédéric
Pitchal; 21, Corbis/Stephane Cardinale; 22, Corbis/Owen Franken; 23t, Shutterstock/Italianestro; 23b, Shutterstock/Saphira;
24, Shutterstock/Stanth; 25, Gordon Joly; 26, Corbis/Gail Mooney; 27, Shutterstock/Derek Gordon;
28, Corbis/Frank Lukasseck; 29t, Corbis/Eric Gaillard; 29b, Björn Appel.

Contents

Discovering France

France is an industrialised nation in western Europe and is almost as big as the US state of Texas. France has a long and rich history. Today it is best known for its fine cuisine, its artistic culture and its beautiful and varied scenery.

The French empire

France has been a major world power for centuries. In 1789, the French Revolution saw the birth of the modern French republic. In the nineteenth century France went on to build one of the world's greatest empires, with colonies in North America and all over Africa.

Today, France still has territories overseas. Guadeloupe and Martinique are two islands in the Caribbean Sea. Réunion is an island off the coast of Madagascar. French Guiana is part of South America. In addition, the Mediterranean island of Corsica is directly ruled by France. These areas are known today as 'overseas departments' of France.

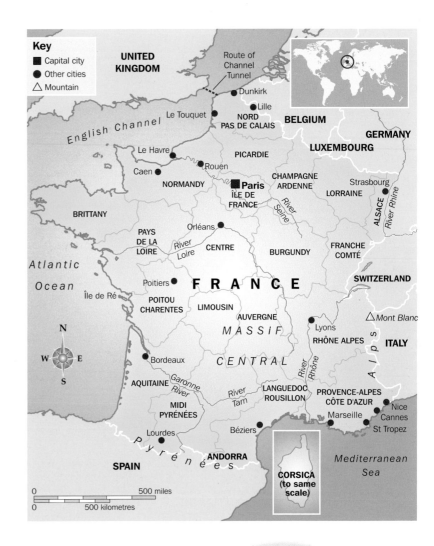

DID YOU KNOW?
The French motto 'Liberté, Égalité, Fraternité' dates back to the French Revolution. Freedom, equality and brotherhood are still important values for all French people.

French rule

During the Second World War (1939-45), France suffered badly under the Nazi occupation. Afterwards, it worked hard to rebuild its economy and infrastructure, and gradually restored relations with Germany.

Today, it is a democratic country with a president and a national legislature. The French people elect a president – currently Nicolas Sarkozy – who serves a five-year term. The president chooses a prime minister to head the government.

France is a founding – and leading – member of the European Union (EU) and has close ties with its European neighbours. EU citizens are allowed to cross European borders freely in search of work, and EU member countries work together at national level to boost trade and raise living standards.

France today

Today the people of France enjoy a relatively stable economy, a high standard of living and generous leisure time. They live in a country with fertile farmland and vineyards, popular mountain ski resorts and beaches on the Mediterranean, Atlantic and northern coasts.

With its rich natural resources and complex and fascinating history, it is no wonder that France is the most visited country in the world, regularly attracting 75 million tourists a year.

France Statistics

Area: 547,030 sq km (211,209 sq miles)

Capital city: Paris

Government type: Republic

Bordering countries: Andorra, Belgium, Germany, Italy, Luxembourg, Monaco, Spain, Switzerland

Currency: Euro (€)

Language: French, plus the following regional dialects and languages: Provençal, Breton, Alsatian, Corsican, Catalan, Basque, Flemish

The Louvre in Paris is the national museum and art gallery of France, and the most visited museum in the world.

Landscape and climate

France is a country of many landscapes, ranging from flat, coastal plains in the north and west, to soaring mountain peaks in the south-east and south-west. With a population of just over 62 million – hardly more than that of the UK – it has a bigger land area than any other country in the EU.

Mountain ranges

France has two major mountain ranges. The Alps, in the south-east of the country, are the most extensive mountain range in Europe and span several countries. The Pyrenees, which are not as high as the Alps, are located in the south-west between France and Spain.

Facts at a glance

Land area: 545,630 sq km (210,669 sq miles)

Water area: 1,400 sq km (540 sq miles)

Highest point: Mont Blanc 4,807 m (15,771 ft)

Lowest point: Rhône River delta (–2m)

Longest river: Loire River, 1,020 km (634 miles)

Coastline: 4,668 km (2,900 miles)

▼ The French Alps are within the regions of Provence-Alpes-Côte d'Azur and Rhône-Alpes. They include Mont Blanc, the highest peak in Europe.

DID YOU KNOW?
Mont Blanc stands directly on the border between France and Italy. Inside it is a 11.6-km (7.2-mile) tunnel that connects the two countries.

France also has smaller mountain ranges and plateaus. Together they form the Massif Central, which covers about 15 per cent of France's land area. This region is good for grazing and its valleys contain much fertile farmland.

Many of France's mountain peaks are covered in snow or glaciers all year round. Some land in the foothills of the mountains is farmed. About one-quarter of France is forest, much of it concentrated in France's mountain regions.

⬥ Vineyards, olive groves and stone-built houses with tiled roofs are typical of the landscape of Mediterranean France.

From mountains to rivers

Mountains affect much of the French landscape and climate. As the weather warms in the spring and summer, the mountain snow melts. It feeds into the five main rivers that meander through the French countryside, the Rhône, Rhine, Seine, Garonne and Loire.

A mild climate

Outside of its mountain regions, France has a generally mild, temperate climate, but freak weather conditions are not unknown. In 2003 a heatwave claimed the lives of nearly 15,000 French people.

The south of France has a Mediterranean climate. Its winters are mild and it is sunny and dry, especially in the summer. Parts of the region are affected by a north wind called the Mistral, which is particularly strong in spring and winter. In the north of the country the climate is colder, but summers are still warm.

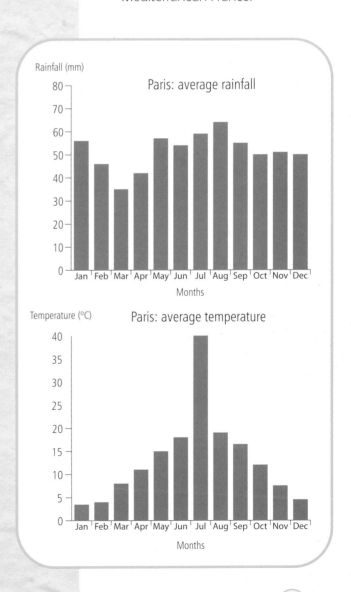

France has the second-highest population in the EU, after Germany. At present births outnumber deaths, and the population is growing slowly but steadily, at around 0.6 per cent each year.

A growing population

At 1.9 children per household, the birth rate in France is one of the highest in the EU. The French government is keen to encourage this trend, as a growing population helps to boost the workforce and create prosperity in years to come.

Facts at a glance

Total population: 62.1 million

Life expectancy at birth:
Male: 77.8 years
Female: 84.3 years

Children dying before the age of five: 0.9%

Ethnic composition: Celtic and Latin with Teutonic, Slavic, North African, Indochinese, Basque minorities

▼ Generous holidays and good working conditions mean that most French people are able to enjoy a more relaxed lifestyle than many of their European neighbours.

Immigration

As well as the high birth rate, the population of France is also growing because of immigration. During the 1950s and 1960s, many immigrants came to France from colonies such as Algeria.

Today more than 7 per cent of the people in France are immigrants. Many are workers from other EU countries. However, compared to other countries in Europe, France has a very low level of immigration, due to the limited number of jobs available.

An ageing population

Because of its high living standards and excellent healthcare, people in France are living longer than ever before. This means that the make-up of the population is changing to include a greater proportion of old people.

By 2030 one in four people in France will be 65 years or older. The result is that younger people who are working will have to pay more tax to pay for healthcare and other services to support the elderly.

Heart disease and cancer

Fewer French people die from heart disease than anywhere else in Europe. However, France has one of the highest rates of cancer in the world, which is the number one cause of death in the country. Almost one in three French people die of cancer.

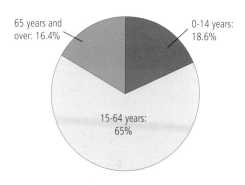

France: age structure of the population

65 years and over: 16.4%

0-14 years: 18.6%

15-64 years: 65%

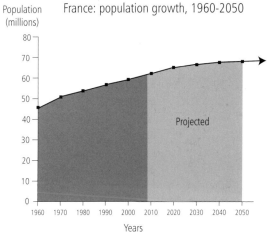

France: population growth, 1960-2050

Population (millions)

Projected

Years

DID YOU KNOW?
On average, French women live for more than 84 years. This is the highest figure for life expectancy in the EU and the second-highest in the world.

▼ A nurse prepares a chemotherapy treatment for a cancer patient at a hospital in Paris.

Settlements and living

Around 77 per cent of the French population live in cities. Over the past 50 years, many people have moved from the countryside to the towns and cities, and the drift to the cities continues. However, France's rural villages and market towns still play a vital part in the economic and cultural life of the country.

The heart of France

With nearly 10 million inhabitants, Paris is by far France's most densely populated city. In central Paris, around 63,000 people are packed into each square mile of the city. Because space is limited, most people live in small apartments.

More than one-tenth of Parisians are foreign-born. The largest immigrant groups are from the North African countries of Algeria, Morocco and Tunisia. Most immigrants live on the outskirts of the city.

DID YOU KNOW?
Since 2002 Paris has had its own artifical beach, complete with sand and deckchairs! 'Paris Plage' on the banks of the Seine has been a big hit with Parisians and tourists.

Situated on the River Seine, Paris is the cultural and commercial heart of France.

Greater Paris

Around 20 per cent of the entire population of France live in 'greater' Paris, which includes the city and surrounding area. Outside the city centre there is more space, so more of the population live in houses rather than flats.

Rural France

The French rural landscape has developed over many centuries and is a patchwork of valleys, vineyards and fertile farmland dotted with small villages. Wealthy city dwellers often have second homes in rural France and move to the country when they retire.

Between 1999 and 2004, many French people moved from cities to the countryside. Most were middle-class commuters and people who were able to use computer links to carry on working away from the city. Some foreigners also settled in rural France to enjoy a better quality of life.

The rural recession

With the decline of farming (see page 22) and the current global recession, many rural communities have been affected by farm closures and job losses. Since 2008, many expatriates who moved to rural France have been forced to return home by the economic downturn.

(see page 22)

Facts at a glance

Urban population: 76.7% (47.6 million)

Rural population: 23.3% (14.5 million)

Population of largest city: 9.9 million (Paris)

▼ Rural France is as important to the country's identity as the Louvre and the Eiffel Tower. This village is in the wine-growing area of Alsace in eastern France.

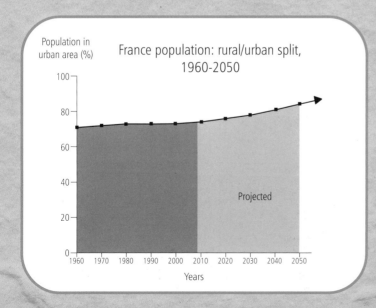

France population: rural/urban split, 1960-2050

Population in urban area (%)

Projected

Years

Family life

In France, the government helps families by providing cheap childcare and by making it easy for mothers to take time off work in order to have babies. Shorter working hours and longer holidays also mean that French families have more time to spend together than in most other EU countries.

Home life

In a typical French family, both partners go out to work during the day, so parents and children mostly spend time together in the evenings, at weekends and in the holidays. Nearly all French families take their summer holidays in August, when many shops and businesses close down altogether.

Facts at a glance

Average children per childbearing woman:
2 children

Average household size:
2.4 people

▼ In order to boost the birth rate, French mothers receive special grants if they have a third child. Larger families also get extra monthly allowances and cheap travel on public transport.

Living apart

Most, but not all, French families are nuclear families. One in six children live with only one parent. One in ten French children grow up in households where one parent has a child from another relationship.

Marriage and 'Pacs'

Although the Catholic Church strongly upholds the value of marriage, most children in France are born to unmarried couples. In fact, only Sweden has fewer marriages than France.

Instead of marriage, some French couples opt for a *pacte civil de solidarité* ('Pac'), which is a legal partnership contract. While half of French marriages end in divorce, only one in seven Pacs are cancelled.

Mixed marriages

About one in seven marriages in France is mixed. This means that one partner is a foreign national. In a mixed marriage, one of the partners is often a migrant worker from another country such as Italy or Spain.

Close to home

Family is highly valued in French society and family members usually like to live close to one another. When young people move away from home, about a quarter of them stay in the same city to be near their family. About half stay in the same region. Often grandparents who live close by help parents by looking after young children and collecting them from school.

⚪ A young French family enjoy a summer break in the mountains.

DID YOU KNOW?
As well as public holidays, full-time workers in France are guaranteed at least five weeks' holiday a year. Many get extra time off if they work more than 35 hours a week.

Religion and beliefs

From 1905 onwards, links between the Catholic Church and the state were formally dissolved and France ceased to have an official religion. Most French people today believe that religious organisations should not be involved in the day-to-day business of running the country.

Main religions

People in France are free to practise any religion. However, more than 80 per cent of French people describe themselves as Roman Catholic and about 15 per cent of French citizens regularly attend religious services. Other religious groups include Muslims, Protestants and Jews.

Research shows that the French are tolerant of other religions. Only 7 per cent of French people would object to their children marrying someone of a different religion to their own.

▼ A Roman Catholic priest celebrates Sunday morning mass at a church in the Burgundy region of east-central France.

Freedom of religion

In recent years, freedom of religion has become a controversial issue in France. In 2004, the government tried to stop the spread of religious fundamentalism in schools by banning the wearing of headscarves, Jewish skullcaps and other 'religious' clothing by students. Ninety per cent of French people supported the government action. However, the new law caused widespread protest, and many Muslims saw it as an attack on important religious freedoms.

Festivals and celebrations

France has 13 public holidays which take place throughout the year. About half of French public holidays are related to the Christian calendar. Easter and Christmas are the most important Christian celebrations.

A uniquely French occasion is Bastille Day which takes place on 14 July every year. On Bastille Day the French remember the Revolution of 1789 with parades and celebrations. On 11 November, Armistice Day, the French remember the 1.5 million French men and women who died in the First World War (1914-18).

⚫ Muslim worshippers in a French mosque. France has a Muslim population of more than 4 million – the largest in Europe. Many are immigrants from former colonies such as Algeria and Morocco.

DID YOU KNOW?
Millions of Christian pilgrims visit Lourdes in the south of France, where spring waters are said to have healing powers. Many sick people claim to have been cured by touching the water.

France: major religions

Atheist: 4%
Jewish: 1%
Muslim: 7%
Protestant: 3%
Orthodox: 1%
Roman Catholic: 84%

Education and learning

All children in France between the ages of six and sixteen have to go to school. Some children aged three to five attend nursery school, but they are not required to by law. Children who attend nursery school often do so because both their parents work.

Types of school

French children attend primary school from six years old to eleven. From eleven to sixteen, they attend *collège* (secondary school). Most children go to state schools, but around 20 per cent of French students attend fee-paying schools, many of which are run by the Catholic Church.

DID YOU KNOW?

Religious education is not taught in French schools. Instead, students have citizenship classes to teach them about the French system of government and how it works.

In French secondary schools, pupils stay in the same class for most subjects rather than being grouped by ability. Class size varies from school to school but is usually between 25 and 30.

Those who do well at school go on to attend an upper secondary school called a lycée until they are eighteen. Unlike A-level students in the UK, they study all kinds of subjects, rather than just a few specific subjects.

French lycée students take exams at the end of each year. In their final year, they sit a Baccalauréat exam. If they pass, they receive a Baccalauréat, or degree. This shows that they have achieved the required standard in a number of subjects and are ready to go to university.

The school day

In French primary schools the day usually starts at 8.30 a.m. and runs until 11.30 a.m., when there is a break for about two hours. Some children go home during the break, but most stay at school for lunch. Lessons begin again at 1.30 p.m. and run until 4.30 or 5.30 p.m. Classes normally last one to two hours.

In most parts of the country, there is no school on Wednesdays, so most French children only attend school for four days a week.

Higher education

Many French students who receive a Baccalauréat go on to university. Others train for a specific job.

The vast majority of French universities are state-funded, and tuition fees for students are low. However, there are also a small number of private colleges and institutes where fee-paying students can study for professional and vocational qualifications.

Facts at a glance

Children in primary school:
Male 99%, Female 99%

Children in secondary school:
Male 98%, Female 100%

Literacy rate (over 15 years):
99%

A cookery demonstration at the École Cordon Bleu, a private training college for chefs in Paris.

Employment and economy

France is one of the world's major economic powers, ranking fifth behind the USA, Japan, Germany and China. At present just over 90 per cent of French people who are able to work are employed. However, like every other EU country, France is being affected by the global recession and unemployment is rising, especially in manufacturing and the retail sector.

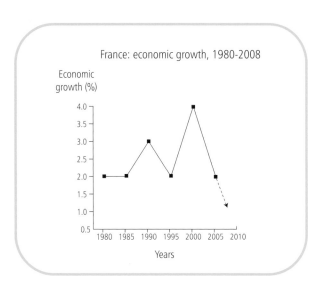

France: economic growth, 1980-2008

Economic growth (%)

Service industry

More than three-quarters of French workers are employed in service industries. These are jobs in which workers take care of people's needs. They include working in restaurants, ski resorts and hotels as well as in hospitals, transport and education.

🔻 Office workers enjoy their lunchtime break in the business and financial district of La Défense in Paris.

French industry

Just under a quarter of French workers are employed in factories making goods such as automobiles, aircraft, electronics, and textiles, or in industries such as food processing.

Until the 1990s many French industries were state-owned, but this has changed. Companies that were once completely owned by the government are now partly or completely owned by private companies. For example, Air France-KLM is almost 20 per cent owned by the French government; 10 per cent of it is owned by its employees and the rest by private investors.

The French government still controls some industries, however, such as power, public transport and defence.

Agriculture

Although only about 4 per cent of French workers are employed in the agricultural sector, French farms still export more agricultural products than any other country in the EU. In fact, France accounts for over 20 per cent of the EU's agricultural output. Its main agricultural products include wine grapes, sugar beets and dairy products.

Facts at a glance

Contributions to GDP:
agriculture: 2%
industry: 21%
services: 77%

Labour force:
agriculture: 4%
industry: 24%
services: 72%

Female labour force:
67.8% of total

Unemployment rate: 8%

◔ Part-owned by the French government, Air France-KLM is one of the world's largest airlines, running passenger and cargo flights to 185 destinations in 83 countries.

DID YOU KNOW?
Writers on France often refer to the years 1945-75 as 'Les trente glorieuses'.* During this time the French economy grew by an average of 6 per cent each year.

* 'The thirty glorious years'

Industry and trade

Most of the money France earns by selling goods abroad comes from manufacturing. The value of the goods that France imports is slightly more than the value of its exports. France trades with 50 countries around the world, but her most important trading partners are other EU countries.

A world leader

France's foreign trade is based on selling high-quality goods such as electronics, aircraft, cars, textiles and processed foods. These products are exported from France all over the world. Since France produces more electricity than it uses, it is also able to sell energy to other countries.

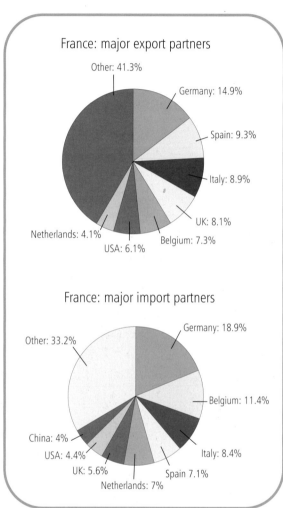

France: major export partners

Other: 41.3%
Germany: 14.9%
Spain: 9.3%
Italy: 8.9%
UK: 8.1%
Belgium: 7.3%
USA: 6.1%
Netherlands: 4.1%

France: major import partners

Other: 33.2%
Germany: 18.9%
Belgium: 11.4%
Italy: 8.4%
Spain 7.1%
Netherlands: 7%
UK: 5.6%
USA: 4.4%
China: 4%

Assembly-line workers build a vehicle at a Renault plant in Caen in northern France. Other important French car manufacturers are Peugeot and Citroen.

Imports

France's chief imports include crude oil, machinery, chemicals and agricultural products. Many of these imports are used to make products that France then exports.

Luxury goods

When people think of France they often think of luxury goods such as fashion, jewellery, perfume and Champagne. Wealthy people all over the world often buy luxury products from France because they are of high quality. French luxury goods are made by highly skilled people, often using rare and expensive materials.

As well as famous French companies such as Cartier, Christian Dior and Chanel, there are many smaller manufacturers of luxury goods. Altogether, the luxury goods industry employs 200,000 people in France.

Technologically advanced

France has some of the world's most advanced technologies. It is a leader in nuclear technology, rapid-transit systems and aircraft design. The French company Airbus is a world leader in making aeroplanes. The French company Renault is the world's fourth-largest car manufacturer, selling 6 million cars in 2008.

As with the luxury industry, many of the leading technology companies in France employ fewer than 100 people. Together, however, they make a big impact on world exports. France is the world's fourth-largest exporter of rubber, chemicals and plastics and the third-largest exporter of pharmaceutical products.

DID YOU KNOW? Fashionable clothes have been a major French export since the seventeenth century. Fashions unveiled on the Paris catwalks set the trends on high streets all over the world.

A model displays the latest styles at a Paris fashion show.

Farming and food

France prides itself on being the world's leading farming and gastronomic nation. As in other EU countries, farming in France has changed greatly over the past 50 years. In 1970, about one-fifth of French workers were in the agricultural sector. Today there are fewer than 600,000 farmers.

A changing world

The fall in the number of farm workers is partly due to increasing mechanisation. As technology has improved, the size of the average farm has increased. At the same time, the total number of farms has fallen.

Facts at a glance

Farmland: 36% of total land area

Main agricultural exports: Beverages, cheese

Main agricultural imports: Animal and vegetable materials, chocolate products

Average daily calorie intake: 3,640 calories

▼ French wine is produced in several regions across the country and makes up 34 per cent of the world market. Once harvested, these grapes will be made into Beaujolais wine.

Farms and vineyards

Almost two-thirds of France's farmland is used for growing crops and the other third for grazing. Cereals such as wheat and barley, root crops such as potatoes and fruits are all produced in great quantities.

Only about 4 per cent of the land is used for vineyards. Even so, France produces more wine than any other country. French wines are considered to be among the best in the world. There are around 500 official wine-makers in France, producing 7 to 8 billion bottles of wine every year.

Food, glorious food

France is known the world over for the quality of its food. Among the most common foods are bread and cheese. Rather than being eaten at the end of a meal, in France cheese is usually eaten before the dessert course.

Bread is a staple part of the French diet, especially at the start of the day, when the French typically eat croissants (crescent-shaped rolls), baguette (a long white crusty loaf) or brioche (a rich bread with added eggs and butter). Bread is bought fresh each day, usually from a local bakery.

The word 'gourmet', meaning 'refined' or 'discerning', is often used to describe French cooking. Dishes such as coq au vin (chicken cooked in wine), boeuf bourguignon (beef stew), ratatouille (vegetable casserole) and bouillabaisse (fish soup) are classic French dishes which are enjoyed all over the world.

DID YOU KNOW?

France's famous post-war leader, General de Gaulle (1890-1970), once said that 'a nation that cannot feed itself cannot be considered great.'

⊙ Onions and garlic are essential ingredients in many famous French dishes.

⊙ With 1,000 varieties to choose from, it is not surprising that French people eat more cheese than any other nation.

Transport and communications

France's internal transport networks are modern and highly efficient. Its road and rail networks also connect with neighbouring countries to make cross-border travel within Europe as quick and easy as possible.

'All roads lead to Paris'

The popular French saying, 'All roads lead to Paris' is partly true. This is because Paris is the major centre for transport n in France. When the French railways were built in the 1800s, they were arranged rather like the spokes of a bicycle wheel, with Paris at the hub.

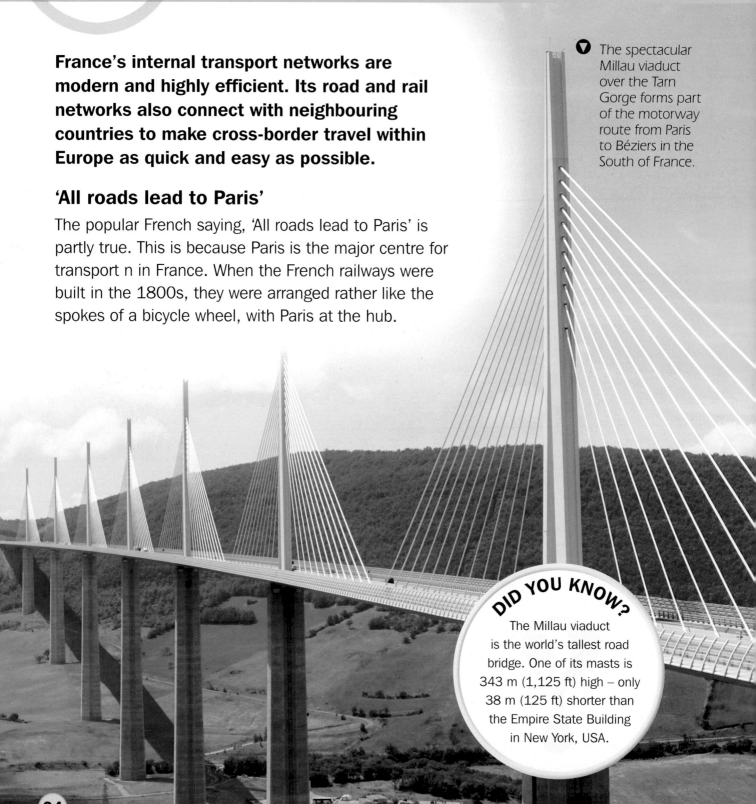

▼ The spectacular Millau viaduct over the Tarn Gorge forms part of the motorway route from Paris to Béziers in the South of France.

DID YOU KNOW?

The Millau viaduct is the world's tallest road bridge. One of its masts is 343 m (1,125 ft) high – only 38 m (125 ft) shorter than the Empire State Building in New York, USA.

When modern roads were first built in the 1900s, the same pattern was followed. Today, one of the challenges the French transport system faces is how to improve services to more remote parts of the country.

High-speed travel

France's high-speed train service is called TGV. The TGV rail network connects many major cities and is one of the most efficient rail services in the world.

Air travel is also fast and reliable. Paris has two main airports, and there are also international airports in Marseilles, Nice, Lille and Strasbourg.

Ports

To transport its goods around the world, France has one of the world's largest merchant fleets. Marseilles is the leading port, but Le Havre, Dunkirk and Rouen are also vital in linking the manufacturing regions of northern France with markets overseas. France's major rivers, the Loire and the Seine, are also important trading routes.

Communicating

There are 80 daily newspapers in France. The French government controls some radio stations and two television stations. This, however, is changing as more channels become privately owned.

Internet use and mobile phones are both common in France. There are more than twice as many mobile phones in use (55 million) as there are landlines (25 million). Roughly half of French households now have Internet access.

⚫ France's record-breaking TGVs are the fastest trains in the world and can reach speeds of 575 kph (357 mph).

Facts at a glance

Total roads: 951,500 km (591,235 miles)

Railways: 29,370 km (18,250 miles)

Major airports: 41

Major ports: 9

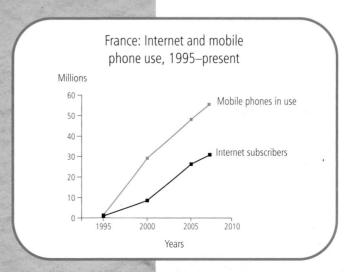

France: Internet and mobile phone use, 1995–present

Leisure and tourism

French people today devote more time to leisure and cultural pursuits than ever before. This is largely due to the shorter working week and the great rise in prosperity which has taken place in the country over the last forty years.

A popular destination

In 2007, France attracted 81.9 million foreign tourists (more than its own population), making it the most popular tourist destination in the world. Paris is the favourite destination for tourists, followed by the Mediterranean coast, where there are many popular beaches and holiday resorts.

Facts at a glance

Tourist arrivals (millions)

1995	60
2000	77.2
2005	75.9
2006	79.1
2007	81.9

▼ The game of boules (bowls) is one of France's most popular pastimes. Results of boules matches are often hotly contested!

Inland tourism

The French often travel within their country, too. Some travel to the coast during the summer to enjoy the beaches or to the mountains in the winter for winter sports. Popular seaside resorts include Saint-Tropez, Cannes and Cap d'Agde on the Mediterranean, Île de Ré and La Baule-Escoublac on the Atlantic coast and Le Touquet on the English Channel.

Free time

The French place a high value on cultural activities and enjoy visiting historic places or museums – especially to see work by famous French artists such as Claude Monet (1840-1926), Paul Cézanne (1839-1906) and Pablo Picasso (1881-1973). One of the largest and most famous art museums in the world is the Louvre in Paris.

The Cité de Sciences et de l'Industrie (City of Science and of Industry) at Le Parc de la Villette in Paris and the Futuroscope theme park near Poitiers also attract large numbers of visitors.

Sport and recreation

France's most popular sport is football. France became the seventh nation to win the football World Cup in 1998, the same year it hosted the event. Tennis is the second most popular sport in France.

Other favourite outdoor activities include cycling, mountain-biking, rock-climbing and cross-country skiing.

⬤ Home to the International Film Festival, Cannes is also one of the country's most popular – and fashionable – holiday resorts.

DID YOU KNOW?
The French language has no word for 'weekend'. Instead, they simply use the English word. This type of borrowing is so common in French it is known as 'franglais'.

Environment and wildlife

Large areas of France are either rural or covered in forest, and much of its wildlife survives in its natural habitat. Some areas are protected from further development, but several animal species remain under threat. At present there are 93 mammal species in France, of which 13 are facing extinction.

Wildlife in France

France's rich wildlife includes wild boar, red deer, wolves, foxes, badgers and chamois. Small mammals include pine martens, red squirrels, hare and lynx.

Facts at a glance

Proportion of area protected: 11.3%

Biodiversity (known species): 5,295

Threatened species: 33

▼ Wild flamingos in the marshy Camargue district of the Rhône delta. The area is also home to many bird species and to roaming herds of wild white horses.

In the last century wolves were hunted to extinction in France. Recently they have re-entered the country from Italy and can be seen again in parts of the Alps.

DID YOU KNOW?
Once extinct in much of Europe, wild boar are common in France. If cornered, a boar will defend itself fiercely. The male lowers his head, charges, and then slashes upward with his tusks.

France's Mediterranean coastline is home to many species of bird. Ducks, geese, starlings, and other birds migrate from northern and eastern Europe to France for the winter. Of France's 269 breeding bird species, seven are endangered.

Fighting climate change

As well as protecting its wildlife, France is taking steps to reduce greenhouse gas emissions and to combat the effects of global warming. At present, France is the EU's main producer of renewable energy such as wind and solar power and produces 15 per cent of Europe's total renewable energy output.

Nuclear energy

France also hopes to reduce harmful emissions by switching from fossil fuels to nuclear power. Since the 1970s, 59 nuclear power stations have been built in France. Altogether, nuclear power stations produce 78 per cent of the country's electricity.

Nuclear energy is clean and does not contribute to carbon emissions, but disposing of nuclear waste is a major problem. The French government has yet to find a method that is completely safe and does not harm the environment.

This solar energy plant in the Pyrenees is the largest of its kind in the world.

Glossary

Catholic Church oldest and largest branch of the Christian community, led by the Pope

climate normal weather conditions of an area

colony a country that is governed and run by another nation

constitution document that sets out the system of laws and government of a country

cuisine food culture of a country

culture way of life and traditions of a particular group of people

delta landform at the mouth of a river

dessert sweet course usually eaten at the end of a meal

economy the way that trade and money are controlled by a country

empire group of countries controlled by a single, more powerful nation

expatriate someone who lives temporarily or permanently in another country

export good or service that is sold to another country

fertile good for growing crops, especially in large quantities

foreign national person who lives in France but is not a French citizen

fundamentalism having extreme or inflexible views

gastronomic dedicated to enjoying food

GDP Gross Domestic Product: the total value of goods and services produced by a country

glacier large, slow-moving body of ice found on land

habitat the place, or type of place, where a plant or animal normally lives

immigration movement of people to a foreign country to live

import good or service that is bought from another country

infrastructure services such as roads, bridges, water and energy that a country needs in order to function

legislature branch of government that makes laws

lycée upper stage of French secondary school system

meander to follow a winding course

merchant fleet ships owned by people that transport goods or other people

metropolitan France the part of the French republic that is located in mainland Europe

migration movement of people from one place to another

natural resources raw materials such as wood and minerals that are found in a country

nuclear energy energy released by a nuclear reaction

nuclear family 'core' family group, usually consisting of father, mother and child(ren)

pharmaceuticals drugs used for medical treatment

plateau a high area of flat ground

private owned by people rather than by the government

republic system of government without a king or queen in which people elect officials to make decisions on their behalf

retail selling goods and products from a shop or store

retire to give up working

rural to do with the countryside or agriculture

sector a division of something such as a type of industry

species group or type of animal or plant

temperate mild climate that is neither extremely hot nor extremely cold

textiles fabric or cloth

unemployment being without paid work

urban to do with towns and town life

Topic web

Use this topic web to explore French themes
in different areas of your curriculum.

History
Find out about the French Revolution. What were some of its causes? How did it change France's relationship with other countries?

Geography
On a map, find one of France's five main river systems. Look at more detailed maps to find out which other rivers and canals are connected to that river system.

Science
Draw a diagram showing a water cycle based on French landscapes such as the Alps, Pyrenees and French rivers.

Maths
The average speed of a TGV is 320 kph (200 mph). How long would it take to travel 640 km (400 miles) on a TGV? How long would it take to travel 1,000 km (625 miles)?

France

English
Some French words and phrases have become common in English. Use a dictionary to find the meaning of the following: *à la carte*, *bon appétit*, *cliché*, *passé*, *vignette*.

Citizenship
What does freedom of religion mean to you? Do you think people should be allowed to wear religious symbols to work and school? Why, or why not?

Design and Technology
Imagine that you work for a Parisian luxury goods company. Draw a design for an item of clothing, a piece of jewellery or a watch.

ICT
Use the Internet to find out more about the Louvre. List some of the famous paintings and artists you could see there.

Further information and index

Further reading

France (Country Topics), Rachel Wright and Anita Ganeri (Franklin Watts 2007)

France (Been There), Annabel Savely (Franklin Watts 2011)

The European Union Today, Simon Ponsford (Franklin Watts 2007)

France (Food and Celebrations), Sylvia Goulding (Wayland 2012)

Web

www.about-france.com

This site contains fast facts and information on French places and culture.

http://news.bbc.co.uk/1/hi/world/europe/country_profiles/998481.stm

This is the BBC news page for France with links to recent events and background information.

Index